This book is dedicated to all my children of light.
May your light shine from above.

-    Your Heavenly Father

CREATIVE NAMES WITH INSPIRATIONAL MEANINGS

LINDA DEAN

iUniverse, Inc.
New York   Bloomington

Creative Names With Inspirational Meanings

iUniverse books may be ordered through booksellers or by contacting:

iUniverse
1663 Liberty Drive
Bloomington, IN 47403
www.iuniverse.com
1-800-Authors (1-800-288-4677)

ISBN: 978-1-4401-1671-1 (pbk)
ISBN: 978-1-4401-1672-8 (ebk)

Printed in the United States of America

iUniverse rev. 12/29/2008

ACKNOWLEDGMENTS

The writing of this book has taken many years of work, reading, and experiences. I have met a lot of people along the way whose' names have intrigued me. I would like to thank God for giving me the patience, determination, persistence and trust in him to complete this book.

I want to thank all the people I've met who have allowed me to use their name in this book.

I also want to thank my children, Kemi, Tierren, and Toiya for contributing names of their friends and acquaintances.

I also give thanks to my family, friends, co-workers and acquaintances for their contribution of names as well.

BOY NAMES
WITH INSPIRITIONAL MEANINGS

A

Aaron (air-ron)	-	Strong willed
Ahmad (ah-mod)	-	Truth bearer
Airnes (air-ness)	-	One who aims high
A'janii (ah-jon-nee)	-	Truly gifted
Ajavon (ah-jah-von)	-	Giving into God
Alex (al-x)	-	One who teaches
Alfonso (al-fon-so)	-	Fisher of men
Alge (al-g)	-	Cornerstone of God
Algernon (Al-ger-non)	-	Giving life
Alif (a-leef)	-	Middle passage
Allen (al-en)	-	Angel of mercy
Alondo (a-lon-do)	-	God sent
Alviston (al-vis-ton)	-	God directed
Alton (al-ton)	-	Wisdom
Amondo (a-mon-do)	-	Anointed to hear from God
Anarie (a-nar-e)	-	Gods increase
Anardo (a-nar-do)	-	Love is
Anfernee (an-fer-nee)	-	Abiding love
Angelo (an-ge-low)	-	Angel of light
Angerico (an-ger-ri-co)	-	One who has a good heart
Antavius (an-tay-vi-ous)	-	Greek emperor
Aramu (ah-rah-mu)	-	Overcoming
Arman (ar-man)	-	God's will
Arnell (ar-nell)	-	God given
Arni (ar-nee)	-	Inspired
Arthur (ar-thur)	-	Expressing all
Arveal (ar-veel)	-	Spiritual growth

Aubrey (au-bree)	-	Awareness
Aundell (aun-dell)	-	Manifest good
Aurek (a-ur-ek)	-	Divine ideas
Austin (aus-tin)	-	Fountain of God
Arzel (r-zel)	-	To reach out
Asim (a-seem)	-	Under God's goodness
Avery (a-ver-e)	-	Happiness
Avishawn (a-vi-shawn)	-	One who is valued
Avonte (a-von-tae)	-	One who is cherished
Axel (ax-l)	-	Inspiration
Ayonte (a-yon-tae)	-	To forgive
Azuwon (a-zu-wan)	-	Spiritual enfoldment

B

Bashawn (bah-shawn)	-	Native son
Baxtron (bax-tron)	-	Ingenuity
Bilal (bih-lah-l)	-	Son of a king
Billard (bil-lard)	-	Positive belief
Ben (b-en)	-	Accomplishment
Benai (ben-I)	-	Father of peace
Benard (ben-ard)	-	First born
Bertram (ber-tram)	-	God's substance
Blair (b-lair)	-	Spiritual gift
Blondell (blon-dell)	-	To know Gods goodness
Bondell (bon-dell)	-	To turn within
Boyd (b-oid)	-	Male pride
Brandon (bran-don)	-	Brave heart
Braxton (brax-ton)	-	The comforter
Brice (br-ice)	-	Good-natured
Brian (bri-an)	-	The lord's gift
Brion (bry-on)	-	Having a servant's heart
Bruce (bru-s)	-	Full of power
Burt (bur-t)	-	Soldier of God
Burtrell (bur-trell)	-	Strong in mind

Bushard (bus-shard)	-	Like God
Byron (by-ron)	-	Great one

C

Ca Darius (kah-dare-e-us)	-	Feeling good
Cael (kay-el)	-	Son of Christ
Caharan (cah-hah-ran)	-	Following Christ lead
Caleb (ca-leb)	-	Following peace
Caliph (Ca-leef)	-	Fathering nations
Calvin (cal-vin)	-	Warrior
Calvonta (cal-von-ta)	-	Grace be to God
Cammeron (cam-er-ron)	-	Humorous
Cantrell (can-trel)	-	To know the Lord
Carl (car-l)	-	Strong rock
Carlos (car-los)	-	powerful
Carnell (car-nel)	-	Peacemaker
Carmien (car-meen)	-	High ruler
Carmon (car-mon)	-	Feeling grateful to God
Caron (car-on)	-	On life's journey
Carter (car-ter)	-	To live abundant
Caterion (kah-teri-on)	-	Favor with God
Caterious (kah-teri-us)	-	Feeling God's nature
Cary (carry)	-	To be a blessing
Cashawn(cash-on)	-	One who is loyal
Chamed (cha-med)	-	Spiritual growth
Chaunce (chon-see)	-	To follow him
Charles (char-rels)	-	Dependable
Chico (che-co)	-	One who is aware
Chris (chris)	-	God's highest creation
Cisco (sis-co)	-	Way maker
Civarino (sih-vah-reno)	-	Creating greatness
Clairon (clar-e-on)	-	Provider
Claudis (clah-dis)	-	To search for goodness
Clayton (clay-ton)	-	Connected to God

Cliffel (clif-fel)	-	Goodness of God
Clinton (clin-ton)	-	God is here
Colby (col-be)	-	Young in spirt
Colin (co-lin)	-	God is available
Collins (cah-lins)	-	Following his goodness
Conoly (con-o-le)	-	Dearly beloved
Corbell (Cor-bell)	-	Prince of peace
Cordell (Cor-del)	-	Peacemaker
Cornell (cor-nel)	-	To find peace
Cory (cor-e)	-	Naturally loved
Courtney (court-nee)	-	God will give peace
Coy (koi)	-	Riches in God
Creflow (creh-flow)	-	To stand in for God
Currell (cure-rell)	-	One who praises God
Curshawn (cur-shawn)	-	To give thanks
Curtell (cur-tel)	-	Greater abundance
Curtis (cur-tis)	-	Forgiveness

D

Daily (day-lee)	-	Under God's leadership
Dale (d-ale)	-	Gentle servant
Dahare (da-har)	-	One who is remembered
Damarko (da-mar-ko)	-	Showing grace
Dameon (day-me-on)	-	Quick and smart
Damian (day-me-an)	-	Courageous one
Darius (dare-e-us)	-	God's partner
Darron (dare-ron)	-	Feeling Gods love
De Armond (dee-are-mond)	-	Under God's wings
Demorio (d-mor-i-o)	-	Forsake not the father
Dequincy (d-quin-see)	-	Warrior in spirit
Damon (day-mon)	-	Fountain of God
Danario (dan-ar-reo)	-	God loves me
D'Angelo (d-an-gelo)	-	Spiritual enfoldment
Daniel (dan-i-el)	-	Brave warrior

Dante (don-tae)	-	Forgiving heart
Danterau (dan-te-ro)	-	Knowing God's way
Dantrell (dan-trel)	-	Child of glory
Darnell (dar-nel)	-	To forgive freely
Darian (dare-e-an)	-	Forever loving God
Darnicious (dar-nih-sious)	-	Forever feeling loved
Darrell (dar-rel)	-	To sing unto the lord
Darrius (dare-e-us)	-	To express all of God
Davell (dah-vell)	-	Needing God's goodness
David (day-vid)	-	To abide in peace
Davie (day-v)	-	True wisdom
Davis (day-vis)	-	Doing good
DaVonte (dah-von-tae)	-	Christ mind
DaVion (day-vi-on)	-	Continued success
Dawan (dah-won)	-	Infinite love
Daymen (Day-men)	-	Ultimate warrior
Dean (d-een)	-	Disciple of truth
Declarence (d-clar-ence)	-	Centered in God
Decuir (dee-cure)	-	Faithfulness
Delonte (del-on-tay)	-	Seeing goodness
Delquan (del-quon)	-	Searching for life
Demaron (d-mar-on)	-	Heading for greatness
Demarco (de-mar-co)	-	Truth, Wisdom & Love
Demetrious (deh-me-tree-ous)	-	Coat of faith
Denardo (d-nar-do)	-	To walk in truth
Dennaris (den-nar-dis)	-	Helping others
Dennis (den-nis)	-	Orderly & Peaceful
Deontha (d-on-tha)	-	New birth
Deontra (d-on-tra)	-	God's will be done
Derik (deh-rick)	-	Giving glory to God
Derrick (deh-rick)	-	God's special child
Deshawn (d-shawn)	-	To manifest God's love
Detwon (det-won)	-	Strength of purpose
DeVaughn (day-von)	-	Under spiritual guidance

Deveon (deh-vee-on)	-	Spreading God's light
Devin (dev-in)	-	Hope & desire
Devion (deh-vee-on)	-	Holding God's hand
Devon (de-von)	-	Meet him at his word.
Deyon (day-on)	-	To overcome limitation
Diamond (dy-mond)	-	Precious jewel
Diamonta (de-ah-monta)	-	Courage
Diswan (dis-wan)	-	To prepare prayerfully
D'jimon (d-jy-mon)	-	Spiritual heritage
Dominic (dom-ih-nick)	-	Doing God's work
Dominique (dom-ih-neek)	-	Golden treasure
Donado (don-a-do)	-	True peace of God
Dondre (don-dray)	-	Determined one
Donnell (don-nell)	-	The word made manifest
Dontae (don-tay)	-	Teaching God's Children
Donyil (don-yil)	-	Conscious awareness
Dorean (dor-ree-an)	-	Filled with grace
Drakahn (dra-kahn)	-	Forever safe in God's arms
Drakon (dra-kon)	-	Finding God's mercy
Dralan (dra-lon)	-	Finding God's goodness
Drewmar (dru-mar)	-	Riches & honor
Drexele (Drex-el)	-	Honoring spirit
Duntrail (dun-trail)	-	Moving in wisdom
Durant (Du-rant)	-	God love's me
Durante' (du-ron-tae)	-	Loving God's mercy
Duron (du-ron)	-	One with success
Duwon (du-won)	-	Thanks be to God
Duwayne (du-wayne)	-	The love of God

E

Edward (ed-ward)	-	Finding God's peace
Efolu (e-fo-lu)	-	Great King
Elden (el-den)	-	Father of love
Elijah (e-li-ja)	-	Great ruler

Elliot (el-li-ot)	-	Newness of life
Ellis (el-is)	-	To know his word
Elondo (e-lon-do)	-	Wings of glory
Elton (el-ton)	-	Finding God's love
Elweth (el-weth)	-	To faint not in well doing
Emeron (eh-mer-on)	-	Power
Emil (e-mil)	-	Gospel
Emon (e-mon)	-	To see God
Enardo (e-nar-doe)	-	Fortune
Enell (e-nel)	-	Spirit sent
Ennis (en-nis)	-	One who overcomes
Enzell (en-zel)	-	One who finds truth
Eric (eh-ric)	-	One who speaks wisdom
Eugene (u-geen)	-	God inspired
Eunicholas (u-nic-koh-las)	-	God given strength
Everard (eh-ver-rard)	-	Fountain of love
Everett (eh-ver-ett)	-	One who is kind
Ethan (e-than)	-	To forgive
Ezell (ez-ell)	-	Coming from God

F

Fabio (fa-bio)	-	Divine mind
Fabrice (fa-breece)	-	Absolute
Faheem (fa-heem)	-	Full of life
Faizon (fay-zon)	-	First cause
Falik (fah-leek)	-	Hope
Faren (fah-ren)	-	Know ye that he is God
Fashard (fah-shard)	-	Mighty Warrior
Fashawn (fah-shawn)	-	Wondrous power
Fellard (fel-lard)	-	To feel deeply
Felon (fel-on)	-	Power and wisdom
Femmeron (fem-mer-on)	-	Universal oneness
Femi (fem-e)	-	God is with me
Ferique (feh-eek)	-	God's infinite knowledge

Ferrel (feh-rel)   -   To lead others
Ferris (ferr-is)   -   Honor and goodwill
Fezel (fee-zel)   -   Voice of Wisdom
Floyd (flo-oid)   -   Messenger of light
Fondell (fon-del)   -   Strength and courage
Fontez (fon-tez)   -   Greatness among men
Fonzeil (fon-zeel)   -   Successful and strong
Frank (f-rank)   -   To win
Fredro (fray-dro)   -   Will power
Freeman (free-man)   -   Honoring God's grace

G

Gabran (ga-bron)   -   A winner
Gabrice (ga-breece)   -   In Gods favor
Gabrion (ga-bre-on)   -   God's disciple
Galeon (gal-e-on)   -   Stable foundation
Garland (gar-land)   -   Peace within
Garret (gair-et)   -   Available to God
Gaston (gas-ton)   -   Strong fighter
Gawon (ga-won)   -   To walk in truth
Geno (jeen-o)   -   One who love's
Gentele' (gen-te-lay)   -   Gentleman
Gerold (geh-rold)   -   Fountain of love
George (g-orge)   -   Man of honor
Germonte (ger-mon-tay)   -   Gift of light
Gervonte' (ger-von-tay)   -   To find truth & wisdom
Gialani (gia-lan-e)   -   Soldier of God
Gian (gee-an)   -   Highly spirited
Gibran (gih-bron)   -   Winning in life
Glen (gah-len)   -   Hard working
Gonda (gon-dah)   -   Father of all men
Gordon (gor-don)   -   Cheerfulness
Grant (ga-rant)   -   A giver
Gregory (gre-gor-e)   -   One who help's

Guerby (ger-bee)	-	Relaxed in God's will
Guiron (gur-on)	-	Life in action
Gunar (gun-ar)	-	Inspired confidence
Guwon (gu-won)	-	Beauty and strength
Guy (gy)	-	Good will

H

Hakan (ha-kon)	-	Showing mercy
Hakeem (ha-keem)	-	Full of goodness
Hakmar (Hak-mar)	-	Obedience to God
Halif (ha-leef)	-	Royal son
Handsome (hand-some)	-	One who looks good
Hank (h-ank)	-	To greet with love
Hampton (hamp-ton)	-	Spiritual melody
Harris (har-ris)	-	King of nations
Harry (hair-ee)	-	God's presence within
Hassan (hah-s-on)	-	Spiritual growth
Hendrick (hend-rick)	-	Armor of God
Hennis (hen-is)	-	God's protecting shield
Henry (hen-ree)	-	To acknowledge God
Herbert (her-bert)	-	Strong and focused
Herman (her-man)	-	Great friend
Hezekiel (heh-ze-kee-l)	-	To bring love
Hilan (hi-lon)	-	One who follows God's will
Hiram (hi-ram)	-	High power
Hombre (om-bray)	-	Man of God
Homer (ho-mer)	-	One who assembles kingdoms
Horace (hor-ace)	-	Energy of love
Hulon (hu-lon)	-	To live by faith

I

Ian (e-an)	-	God's will
Innis (In-nis)	-	Abiding in grace

Ira (I-rah)	-	God sent
Irie (I-ree)	-	Learning to love
Irving (erv-ing)	-	One with happiness
Isaac (i-zak)	-	Laughter
Isaiah (I-say-ah)	-	Great prophet
Ivan (I-van)	-	To feel strength
Ivar (I-var)	-	One with great strength

J

Ja Brawn (ja-bron)	-	The final word
Jacques (ja-kees)	-	Love of water
Jaden (jay-den)	-	Star child
Jadrien (ja-dreen)	-	Visionary
Jaheim (ja-heem)	-	True light of love
Jahliv (ja-leev)	-	To prepare for God
Jairus (jy-rus)	-	Trusting in God
Jaive (ja-vay)	-	To sit with God
Jakobe (jah-ko-be)	-	Loving under God
Jakove' (ja-ko-vay)	-	Setting the standard
Jalen (jay-len)	-	Singing God's praises
Jalil (jah-lill)	-	True mercy
Jamad (jah-mod)	-	Peace offerings
Jamal (jah-mall)	-	Finding God's way
Jamani (jah-mon-nee)	-	Beauty and majesty
Jamar (jay-mar)	-	Son of man
Jamarious (jah-mar-re-us)	-	Shining God's light
Jamauri (jah-mah-ree)	-	Having God's strength
Jamerio (jah-merry-o)	-	The great one
James (james)	-	The living God
Jamil (jah-mill)	-	Close to God
Jancer (jan-ser)	-	speaking forgiveness
Jaquan (jah-quan)	-	Feelings of Goodness
Jaquil (jah-keel)	-	One with authority
Jared (jaa-red)	-	Finishing God's work

Jaren (jar-en)	-	God's message
Jarmani (jar-mon-nee)	-	Majesty
Jarron (jar-on)	-	God's loving way
Jairus (jy-rus)	-	Author of faith
Jarai (jah-ry)	-	Favoring goodness
Jarquavious (jar-quay-ve-us)	-	Model of God
Jarvis (jar-vis)	-	Singleness of faith
JaSiel (jah-seel)	-	God expresses through me
Jason (jay-son)	-	Light of love
Jaunell (jon-ell)	-	Disciple of love
Javelle (jah-vell)	-	Working with God
Javion (jay-ve-on)	-	To master love
Javon (jah-von)	-	Under God's peace
Jawand (jah-wand)	-	Walking in God's love
Jawon (jah-won)	-	A mother's joy
Jay (J)	-	A great speaker
Jaydinn (jay-din)	-	Finishing God's Word
Jaylan (jay-lan)	-	A solid foundation
Jaymar (jay-mar)	-	To find peace
Jeffrey (jeff-ree)	-	One who builds
Jean-Jaques (jon-jocks)	-	Wisdom
Jemal (jee-mall)	-	Following God's word
Jerel (jeh-rell)	-	Worthy of honor
Jeremiah (jeh-reh-my-ah)	-	Great priest
Jermonte (jer-mon-t)	-	A survivor
Jerod (jeh-rod)	-	A father's pride
Jeson (jay-son)	-	Willing to learn
Jevon (jeh-von)	-	Learning to love
John (jon)	-	Witness to the light
Johnelle (john-el)	-	Truly giving
Joloni (jo-lon-e)	-	Saving grace
Jonte' (john-tay)	-	Full of wisdom
Jordan (jor-dan)	-	Majestic and mighty
Joshawn (jo-shon)	-	God's unfailing love
Joshua (josh-u-ah)	-	Salvation cometh

Jubril (ju-brill)	-	Giving kindness
Juliano (ju-le-on-o)	-	I come in peace
Julius (ju-le-us)	-	Prince of love
Justin (jus-tin)	-	Prosperity of God
Justtyn (jus-tin)	-	Wonderful man
Juwan(ju-won)	-	The breath of freedom

K

Kamal (kah-mall)	-	Remembering God's favor
Kamau (kah-ma-oo)	-	Silent Warrior of God
Keely (kee-lee)	-	Going forward in truth
Keenan (kee-nan)	-	Strong and courageous
Kefla (kef-lah)	-	Many blessings
Kehinde (kay-hin-day)	-	Dwelling in peace
Keion (key-on)	-	Goodness and mercy
Keir (keer)	-	Coming closer to God
Keith (keeth)	-	To dwell in God's presence
Keldon (kel-don)	-	Positive and unique
Kenyon (ken-yon)	-	Filled with grace and love
Keon (key-on)	-	To find love
Keontre (key-on-tray)	-	Expressing God's glory
Keyaan (key-an)	-	Founder of love
Keynan (key-nan)	-	Warrior for God
Keyon (key-on)	-	Surrounded by grace
Kelly (kel-lee)	-	God is with me
Kelon (key-lon)	-	One who forgives
Kelsy (kel-sea)	-	The indwelling presence
Kennard (ken-nard)	-	God's gift
Kervin (ker-vin)	-	Love and family
Kerwin (Ker-win)	-	To lift up the son
Keshane (kee-shane)	-	To finish strong
Keshawn (key-shon)	-	To move forward
Kevin (keh-vin)	-	To hold on to love
Kewan (key-won)	-	First son

Keyshawn (Key-shon)	-	To follow through
Kezzie (kez-zee)	-	Back to life
Khaalid (kah-lid)	-	Born into wealth
Khalil (kah-lil)	-	Following love
Khamani (kha-mah-nee)	-	Meaningful love
Khiry (khir-ree)	-	Under the spirit of God
Kierren (khir-ren)	-	Prayer warrior
Kindrick (kin-drick)	-	Feeding on God's word
Kilwon (kil-won)	-	One who is lifted up
Kiford (khi-ford)	-	The law of the lord
Kirtrell (khir-trell)	-	God makes a way
Kisel (kiss-el)	-	To be still and know
Kitrell (kit-rell)	-	To enjoy peace
Kinell ((kin-ell)	-	Oneness with God
Kody (ko-dee)	-	Wayshower
Kofe (ko-fay)	-	To find love
Kozel (ko-zell)	-	Stands firm on truth
Kurt (kur-t)	-	Our Beloved
Kyle (khy-l)	-	Unified love
Kyon (kee-on)	-	One who sings praises

L

Ladarian (lah-dare-ian)	-	To dwell in Gods presence
LaDatrian (lah-da-tree-an)	-	To grow in prosperity
LaDerrick (lah-der-rick)	-	Having qualities of God
LaKowon (lah-kwon)	-	God is my source
Lamar (lah-mar)	-	God is my life
LaMarcus (lah-mar-cus)	-	The power of strength
Lamon (lah-mon)	-	Finding peace in God
Laronzo (lah-ron-zoe)	-	Perfection
La Shaun (lah-shawn)	-	God's leader
Lance (lance)	-	To put God first
Lando (lan-doe)	-	To have happiness
Landon (land-on)	-	To have wisdom

Lanell (lah-nell)	-	To dwell in goodness
Larenz (lah-renz)	-	Forever faithful
Larmis (lar-mis)	-	God revealed
Larnell (lar-nell)	-	Thy will be done
Larry (larr-ree)	-	Leaning on God
LaQuain (lah-quane)	-	Showing God's mercy
Laquavious (la-quay-vi-ous)	-	One who rules
LaShay (lah-shay)	-	Shining light
Latheris (lah-their-is)	-	One who is divinely guided
Latrell (lah-trell)	-	One who understands
LaVon (lah-von)	-	The hand of the lord
LaVar (lah-var)	-	The savior
Lawayne (lah-wane)	-	One who guards and protects
Ledell (lah-dell)	-	Trust & confidence
Lemond (lay-mond)	-	The honor of God
Leonard (leo-nard)	-	One who is grateful to God
LeVon (lay-von)	-	God filled.
Lindell (lin-dell)	-	One who is balanced
Liston (lis-ton)	-	Free-flowing love
Luther (lu-ther)	-	To walk in the light.
Lyle (lye-l)	-	One who sends joy.
Lynoy (lyn-oy)	-	To rejoice in God
Lyreo (lih-ray-o)	-	God created

M

Madicke (mah-dee-kay)	-	Forming greatness
Makai (mah-kye)	-	Glorious in battle
Malcom (mal-come)	-	Belonging to God
Mali (mah-lye)	-	Feeding my faith
Malik (mah-leek)	-	native son
Marcel (mar-cell)	-	One who is noble
Marcio (mar-see-o)	-	Filled with passion
Marcus (mar-cus)	-	Vibrant one
Mardell (mar-dell)	-	Turning to God
Mario (mar-e-o)	-	Center of God's love

Marlon (mar-lon)	-	Gods word
Marnell (mar-nell)	-	Same as God
Marquavious (mar-quay-vee-us)	-	Sharing goodness
Marquis (mar-kees)	-	Filled with the spirit
Marshal (mar-shall)	-	Love unconditional
Marshawn (mar-shawn)	-	Self-confidence
Marshique (mar-sheek)	-	To draw forth
Martavious (mar-ta-vi-ous)	-	No truth untold
Marvis (mar-vis)	-	To express God
Marvin (mar-vin)	-	To love people
Maudarious (ma-dar-e-us)	-	Following God's Presence
Mekhi(meh-ky)	-	Following truth
Melvin (mel-vin)	-	To show love
Michael (my-kel)	-	Powerful
Milan (mih-lon)	-	To work by grace
Milani (mih-lon-ni)	-	To call forth peace
Miles (mile-s)	-	Potential for greatness
Maurice (mau-reece)	-	God is the way
Moise (mo-ese)	-	Tuning into light
Montell (mon-tell)	-	Continued hope
Montez (mon-tez)	-	Showered with blessings
Montorious (mon-tor-ree-us)	-	Seeing God's goodness
Morgan (mor-gan)	-	To call forth love
Morris (mor-ris)	-	Unified Love
Mylan (mi-lan)	-	Under God's grace

N

Naequan (nay-qwon)	-	Grateful heart
Najja (nah-ja)	-	Under God's prescence
Nakwan (nah-kwon)	-	Leadership
Nalik (nah-leek)	-	God operates in me
Narcell (nar-cell)	-	He who is created of God
Narlan (nar-lan)	-	God is greatness
Narris (nar-ris)	-	Destiny
Nashawn (nah-shawn)	-	The substance of God

Nartell (nar-tell)	-	I am health
Narvin (nar-vin)	-	God is everywhere
Naseem (nah-seem)	-	Great giver
Nathan (nay-than)	-	Turn to God first.
Navonte (nah-von-tey)	-	Greatness within
Neal (nee-l)	-	The wisdom of God
Nelson (nel-son)	-	One who gives
Nevon (neh-von)	-	Goodness and mercy forever
Nicholas (nih-co-las)	-	To stand for truth
Nigel (ny-gel)	-	Good natured
Noel (no-el)	-	One who speaks the truth
Nolan (no-lan)	-	One who reflects inner peace
Norman (nor-man)	-	A trailblazer
Norris (nor-ris)	-	I receive love
Nymrod (nym-rod)	-	God guides me

O

Obari (o-bar-e)	-	One with wisdom
Octavious (oc-tay-vi-ous)	-	Feeling secure
Odell (o-dell)	-	Provider
Ogbonna (og-bonna)	-	Young warrior
Olan (o-lan)	-	To believe
Oliver (ah-li-ver)	-	Wonderful work of God
Omar (o-mar)	-	To receive love
Omari (o-mar-e)	-	True gift of love
Omarion (o-mar-e-on)	-	Giving peace and love
O'neal (o-neel)	-	Strengh & Power
Orenthal (o-ren-thal)	-	Justice
Orlando (or-land-o)	-	To find God's treasure
Oscar (os-car)	-	To dream big
Oshawn (0-shawn)	-	To do Gods work
Oshay (o-shay)	-	Forming wisdom
Otis (o-tis)	-	Willing servant

P

Page (p-age)	-	To think young
Pascal (pass-cal)	-	Giving hope
Patrick (pat-rick)	-	Voice of God
Paul (p-all)	-	Apostle of God
Pavilon (pah-vil-e-on)	-	Anointed by God
Perrick (pehr-rick)	-	Blessed one
Perry (pehr-ree)	-	Under God's command
Peter (pee-ter)	-	Faith
Pharell (pha-rel)	-	To open up to God
Pheodus (phe-o-dus)	-	God leads
Phyllip (phih-lip)	-	God is with me
Pierce (peer-s)	-	Flowing in love
Praise God (prays-god)	-	High honor
Prashendall (prah-shen-dall)	-	Truly guided
Prentice (pren-tis)	-	New thought
Preston (pres-ton)	-	God be with you
Prince (prin-s)	-	Gods royalty

Q

Quadarius (qua-dar-e-ous)	-	Conquering spirit
Quadree (qua-dree)	-	Sharing God's goodness
Quan (qoo-on)	-	Father of light
Quondre (qoo-on-dray)	-	To live in God's presence
Quantaveous (qoo-on-tay-ve-us)	-	Favoring peace
Quartez (qu-ar-tez)	-	Finally free
Quentin (quen-tin)	-	Godliness
Quenton (quen-ton)	-	God answers
Quincy (quin-see)	-	God knows me
Quintrail (quin-trail)	-	God as me
Qumar (q-mar)	-	God takes care

R

Raekwon (ray-kwon)	-	To lean on God
Ralpheal (rah-phee-al)	-	Moving together in love
Ranada (rah-nah-dah)	-	To run free
Rance (ran-c)	-	God's witness
Randy (ran-dee)	-	Gentle spirit
Ranon (rah-non)	-	Knowing God's purpose
Rashawn (rah-shon)	-	Gods holy spirit
Rashid (rah-sheed)	-	To send great love
Raswan (rah-swan)	-	To think of love
Ravaughn (rah-von)	-	Searching for truth
Ravelle (rah-vel)	-	To honor God
Raymond (ray-mond)	-	God send
Raymont (ray-mont)	-	Native spirit
Reed (reed)	-	Mighty God
Reggie (reh-gee)	-	To see things as they are
Renard (re-nard)	-	One who is grounded
Reno (re-no)	-	Fondness
Rexon (rex-on)	-	God comes with me
Ricardo (re-car-do)	-	God of all
Richard (rich-ard)	-	Right to prosperity
Ricky (rick-e)	-	Love of family
Robert (rob-ert)	-	Loving nature
Rodarian (ro-dare-e-an)	-	Power from God
Roderick (rod-er-rick)	-	Full of light
Rodger (rod-ger)	-	Coming together
Rommell (ro-mel)	-	Anchored in God
Ronell (ron-el)	-	One who spreads love
Ronny (ron-e)	-	Pure joy
Ronsard (ron-sard)	-	Forever with God
Roric (ror-ic)	-	To feel truth
Rosco (ros-co)	-	To live in truth
Roy (roi)	-	To see truth
Royan (roy-an)	-	To have God's strength

Rushawn (ru-shon)	-	To live in prosperity
Russell (rus-sel)	-	Speak truth
Ryan (ry-an)	-	To follow God's way

S

Sakeem (sah-keem)	-	Sacred heart
Sam (s-am)	-	One who is merciful
Samari (sah-mar-e)	-	Understanding God's love
Savior (sa-vi-or)	-	To feel loved
Scott (scot)	-	Loving manchild
Sentall (sen-tall)	-	First child
Seven (sev-en)	-	Spiritual nature
Shales (shay-ls)	-	One who is giving
Shamar (sha-mar)	-	One with light
Shane (shay-n)	-	Growing in love
Shante (shon-tay)	-	A willing heart
Shaquil (sha-quil)	-	Strength of mind
Shatray (sha-tray)	-	Final authority
Shavon (shay-von)	-	To love
Shawn (shaw-n)	-	Building courage
Shayaa (shay-ah)	-	Praised by God
Shatwan (sha-twan)	-	God filled
Shorro (shor-ro)	-	Giving light unto humanity
Sidarrius (sih-dari-us)	-	Born king
Sidney (sid-ney)	-	Knowing God's love
Simal (sih-mall)	-	Calm peace
Simeon (sih-meon)	-	My soul gives
Sivon (sih-von)	-	Coming from God
Skylar (sky-lar)	-	God's source for love
Skyro (sky-ro)	-	God is my strength
Sledge (sled-ge)	-	Feeling peace within
Sonel (so-nell)	-	God's son arrives
Sonny (son-e)	-	Finding truth
Spencer (spen-cer)	-	Unique spirit

Stacato (sta-cah-toe)	-	Following God's wisdom
Starjoe (star-joe)	-	Forever blessed
Stefahn (steh-fawn)	-	Life gives unto me
Stephen (steh-phen)	-	Life gives me plenty
Sutton (sut-ton)	-	Success is mine
Syrus (sye-rus)	-	Received with love

T

Taaron (taa-ron)	-	To teach God's love
Tacarry (tah-carry)	-	To feel God's love
Tahary (tah-harry)	-	God's spirit to all
Tahiem (tah-heem)	-	God's giving spirit
Tahjee (tah-jee)	-	To know God's love
Tajh (taj)	-	Coming to God
Taji (taj-e)	-	Sharing God's wealth
Takeo (tah-ke-o)	-	finding God's wisdom
Tamar (tah-mar)	-	Teaming with God
Tamion (tay-me-on)	-	One who sees blessings
Taraun (taa-run)	-	Soothing nature
Tarmell (tar-mell)	-	Tender mercies
Tarvel (tar-vel)	-	Under God's care
Tashard (tah-shard)	-	God of light
Tavare (tah-var-e)	-	To show God's grace
Tavious (tay-ve-us)	-	Honoring God's wisdom
Taylen (tay-len)	-	Feeling strong
Tavon (tay-von)	-	Under the will of God
Teneron (ten-eh-ron)	-	Holding onto faith
Terence (terr-ence)	-	To give thanks
Terrell (ter-rel)	-	God leads
Terron (terr-on)	-	God hath given
Tier (teer)	-	Blessed
Tierren (teer-ren)	-	Powerful one
Timothy (ti-mo-thy)	-	To trust the inner God
Tom (t-om)	-	God's guidance

Tonell (toe-nel)	-	Created of God
Tonai (toe-nye)	-	I receive life
Tony (tone-nee)	-	Coming forth from the center
Tor (t-or)	-	He is king
Torrell (tor-rell)	-	To find power
Tracy (tray-see)	-	Peace & stillness
Treandos (tree-an-dos)	-	Finding life through love
Trello (trel-lo)	-	Under God's care
Tre'marr (tray-mar)	-	God sent
Tre'mont (tray-mont)	-	Spiritual
Trenovion (tren-no-vion)	-	Holding onto God
Trent (tren-t)	-	God empowers me
Trevaris (tray-var-is)	-	God's divine heir
Tre'von (tray-von)	-	One with affection.
Trey (tray)	-	One who instructs
Triano (tree-ah-no)	-	Peace-filled
Trinity (trin-ih-t)	-	Taking charge
Troy (troy)	-	One who gives understanding
Terfa (ter-fah)	-	God knows
Tyjuan (ty-won)	-	Love & peace
Tyler (ty-ler)	-	Born again
Tyquan (tye-kwon)	-	God natured
Tyrel (ty-rel)	-	Son of God
Tyrice (tye-reece)	-	New life
Tyrone (tye-rone)	-	Eyes of love
Tyvar (ty-var)	-	Under God's love
T'ziah (t-zy-ah)	-	Unified truth

U

Udonis (u-don-is)	-	Giving great love
Ulan (u-lon)	-	Universal love
Ulner (ul-ner)	-	Universal force
Ulric (ul-rick)	-	Tuning into God
Umar (you-mar)	-	Universal energy

Umil (you-mil)	-	Positive vision
Unell (u-nell)	-	To follow my word
Ungar (un-gar)	-	Spiritual Understanding
Uriel (u-reel)	-	Unspoken love
Ushaun (u-shawn)	-	Joy and peace
Usher (us-sher)	-	God inspired
Utahn (u-tawn)	-	Boundless wisdom
Unoris (you-nor-is)	-	Understanding love

V

Vabrice (vah-breece)	-	To trust in God
Valiant (vali-ent)	-	Prince of faith
Vanar (van-ar)	-	To magnify God's presence
Vance (van-s)	-	To be blessed
Varian (vaar-ian)	-	To trust God completely
Vario (var-e-o)	-	God directed
Vaughn (von)	-	God counsels
Venar (ven-ar)	-	Love & praise
Viceto (vih-cet-o)	-	To focus on God
Victor (vic-tor)	-	To be kind
Vimar (vim-ar)	-	Under God's guidance
Vincent (vin-cent)	-	One who touches the heart
Vishawn (vih-shon)	-	One with high vision

W

Wade (wade)	-	God is my source
Walter (wal-ter)	-	Rivers of love
Wari (war-e)	-	Family first
Warren (war-ren)	-	To love someone
Warrik (war-ik)	-	Spirit of love
Wayland (way-land)	-	Removed from harm
Wayne (way-ne)	-	Angels watching over me
Wesley (wes-lee)	-	A royal heir

Willard (wil-lard)	-	Givingness
William (willie-um)	-	To call forth love
Winston (wins-ton)	-	Connected to God
Wundu (wun-du)	-	Living in Wisdom

X

Xaun(x-on)	-	God's creation
Xavier (x-a-v-er)	-	God's hope
Xilar (x-ilar)	-	To know I'm loved

Y

Yancy (yan-cee)	-	One who is proud
Yinzell (yin-zell)	-	The highest and best
Yitrell (yih-trel)	-	Born to succeed
Yonar (yo-nar)	-	Love everlasting
Yonell (yo-nell)	-	A spiritual being
Yoner (yo-ner)	-	Born to learn
Yonzel (yon-zel)	-	A blessing to all
Yunar (you-nar)	-	Following God's path

Z

Zanar (zan-ar)	-	Born into pure spirit
Zantrel (zan-trel)	-	Grounded in goodness
Zavon (zay-von)	-	Loving God's wisdom
Zenil (zen-il)	-	Coming from the father
Zierren (zeer-ren)	-	God's generosity
Ziron (zy-ron)	-	Divine love
Zitahn (zit-ahn)	-	One who gives God's love
Zoe (zo-e)	-	One who sees beyond life
Zonar (zo-nar)	-	Thy will be done
Zoron (zor-ron)	-	Increased faith

GIRL NAMES
WITH INSPIRATIONAL MEANINGS

A

Ache' (ah-chay)	-	Under God's wisdom
Adaora (ah-dor-ah)	-	Restoration power
Adore (ah-dor)	-	To wait on spirit
Adia (ah-dee-ah)	-	Under divine love
Adria (a-dree-ah)	-	To move in spirit
Aisha (ah-e-sha)	-	Life
Aja (ah-ja)	-	Light of life
Ajale' (ah-ja-lay)	-	Open to God
Ajiah (ah-g-ah)	-	Faithful heart
Akeelah (ah-kee-lah)	-	Guiding light
Akiela (ah-kee-lah)	-	Native girl
Akilah (ah-kee-lah)	-	Under God's shadow
Akisha (ah-kee-sha)	-	Loved by God
Akita (ah-kee-tah)	-	Joyous love
Aldena (al-dee-nah)	-	Love
Aleana (ah-leena)	-	Pleasing God
Alencia (ah-lencia)	-	God is
Alexandrea (alex-an-dree-ah)	-	Woman of vision
Alexis (ah-lexis)	-	To love
Alia (ah-lee-ah)	-	Heart of God
Alijah (a-lee-jah)	-	God's choice
Alju (al-ju)	-	Finding spiritual truth
Almonetta (al-mon-etta)	-	Love of life
Alonia (ah-lon-e-ah)	-	Sincerely loved
Altamesa (al-tah-may-sah)	-	To seek God always
Altina (al-tina)	-	One who listens
Alvatina (al-vah-tina)	-	One who loves God

Alyse (al-ees)	-	God protects me
Ambria (am-bre-ah)	-	Following God's principals
Amelita (ah-meh-leta)	-	move close to God
Amenia (ah-menia)	-	Back to life
Anastasia (an-as-stasia)	-	God loves you
Angerica (an-geri-cah)	-	Angel of love
Anika (ah-nee-kah)	-	Brave one
Allison (alice-son)	-	God's chosen one
Anisha (an-ih-sha)	-	To help others
Anissa (ah-nis-ah)	-	Pleasing to God
Anitra (ah-nee-tra)	-	Lovely one
Anjeanette (an-jean-ette)	-	The meaning of love
Angelyn (an-geh-lyn)	-	Years of growth
Anneshia (ann-e-she-ah)	-	To glorify God's presence
Annette (ann-ette)	-	Following God's presence
Anntrina (ann-trina)	-	Gifted
Anntrita (ann-tri-ta)	-	Success in God
Anteidra (an-tee-dra)	-	Showing kindness
Antonette (an-ton-ette)	-	Peacemaker
Aquenetta (ah-quen-ette)	-	Serious one
Arcadia (ar-cade-ia)	-	Warm heart
Arcavia (ar-cay-via)	-	Foundation of wealth
Arenthia (ah-ren-thia)	-	Glowing with goodness
Ariel (ar-e-l)	-	Gods child
Ariela (ar-e-ella)	-	To make peace
Arleatha (ar-lee-tha)	-	God's sunshine
Armica (ar-me-kah)	-	Giving Gods Love
Arnetra (ar-nee-tra)	-	Belonging
Artice (ar-teese)	-	One who leads
Articia (ar-tih-sha)	-	Love of art
Artina (ar-tina)	-	moving in grace
Ashane' (ah-sha-nay)	-	Warm and sincere
Ashanta (ah-shon-tah)	-	Truly wonderful
Ashanti (ah-shon-ti)	-	Glorious wonder

Ashley (ash-lee)	-	Royalty
Astrid (as-trid)	-	Proud
Aubrey (au-bree)	-	One who teaches
Audrina (aud-rina)	-	God's child
Aunjanae (aun-ja-nae)	-	Inspired love
Avianne (a-vi-anne)	-	Strong and pretty
Ayonna (a-yon-na)	-	God's spirit
Azungwe (ah-zun-gway)	-	God have mercy
Azurinthia (ah-zu-rin-thia)	-	Climbing to the top

B

Banita (bah-nita)	-	Glorious
Barbara (bar-ba-ra)	-	To hear from God
Belma (bel-ma)	-	Fire
Bertha (ber-tha)	-	Strong one
Bertice (ber-tice)	-	Strong in knowledge
Bevelyn (beh-veh-lyn)	-	God's glory to all
Bianca (b-on-kah)	-	Sincere and sweet
Byonce' (b-on-say)	-	Loveliness
Boniqua (bo-ne-quah)	-	Love song
Bonnie (bon-nee)	-	Blessed with humor
Brandy (bran-d)	-	Talented one
Breahna (bre-ah-nah)	-	To have God's glory
Brianna (bre-anna)	-	Cute
Brigit (bri-git)	-	Genius
Brina (bre-nah)	-	Love and Wisdom
Brittany (brit-tany)	-	Renewed Spirit
Bryann (bre-ann)	-	Great one

C

Calcaneous (cal-kane-e-us)	-	Spirit of God
Calisa (cah-lih-sah)	-	Glowing
Camara (cam-ah-rah)	-	Sent from God to prosper.

Camera (cam-er-ah)	-	Finding truth within
Camry (cam-ree)	-	One with style
Candice (can-dis)	-	Spiritual light
Canice (can-dis)	-	Following the word of God
Canisius (cah-nih-se-us)	-	Honoring the word of God
Capricia (cah-pre-see-ah)	-	Intelligent one
Capucine (cah-pu-seen)	-	Faith centered
Carlesheia (car-lesh-ia)	-	Harmonious
Carletta (car-letta)	-	Loving
Carmen (car-men)	-	Sweet one
Carolyn (caro-lyn)	-	To give love
Carmelita (car-meh-lita)	-	God's image
Carshena (car-she-nah)	-	To love God
Casandra (cah-san-dra)	-	Special one
Cashey (cah-she)	-	Graceful and calm
Cathena (cah-thee-na)	-	Living life with purpose
Catima (cah-tee-ma)	-	Loving nature
Catreka (cah-tree-kah)	-	Pure love and peace
Celeste (ce-lest)	-	Angel
Celisse (ce-liss)	-	Coming to the Lord
Centerial (cen-teri-al)	-	Finishing with greatness
Chakisha (cha-kee-sha)	-	Light of dawn
Chalaundria (cha-laun-dria)	-	To glory in God's presence
Chandra (chan-dra)	-	Life-giving
Chandria (chan-dre-ah)	-	Mothering nature
Chandrica (chan-dree-kah)	-	Forgiving
Chanell (cha-nell)	-	Sweetness
Chanesa (cha-nee-sah)	-	Delicate
Chanaye (cha-nay)	-	Confident
Chantel (chon-tel)	-	Seeing God's grace
Charmel (char-mel)	-	Guiding light from God
Charneeta (char-nee-tah)	-	Mother & Father love
Chasidy (cha-sidy)	-	True spirit of God
Chaunita (chon-nita)	-	Cool one

Chauntay (chon-tay)	-	Goddess
Chenica (che-ni-kah)	-	Gods light
Chequita (che-kee-tah)	-	Loving spirit
Cheron (che-ron)	-	Glowing with love
Chevelta (cheh-vel-tah)	-	Leading the way of truth
Chiketa (chi-kee-tah)	-	sunshine and glory
Chiree (chih-ree)	-	Peace and poise
Chrishma (chrish-mah)	-	Caring for all
Christeta (chris-teh-tah)	-	Christ child
Chrysti (chris-tee)	-	All that is good
Chyna (chy-na)	-	Feeling God's spirit
Cilene (ci-leen)	-	Willing to give
Clinique (clih-neek)	-	Loving grace
Cloie (clo-e)	-	Lucky one
Concetta (con-cet-tah)	-	Miracle child
Corlyn (cor-lyn)	-	Fun loving
Coryn (cor-in)	-	To generate love
Courtney (cort-ney)	-	Heavenly
Cree (kree)	-	Honoring truth
Cynne' (cyn-nay)	-	Wonderful love
Cyrah (cy-rah)	-	Royal one
Cyrea (cy-rea)	-	Princess
Cyrena (cy-re-nah)	-	Graceful
Cytiya (cih-ty-ah)	-	To give strength

D

Dachal (da-chal)	-	Full of wonder
Dalene (dah-leen)	-	Growing with God
Dameda (dah-me-dah)	-	Gods chosen one
Damica (dah-me-cah)	-	To go with love
Damika (dah-me-kah)	-	Strong character
Damita (dah-me-tah)	-	Gods grace
Danada (dah-nah-dah)	-	One who is thankful
DaNae (dah-nay)	-	To be true

Danielle (dan-e-l)	-	To be loved
Danika (dan-e-kah)	-	Joy
Danisha (dan-e-sha)	-	To have fame
Danterian (dan-teh-re-an)	-	To feel God's power
Danyl (dan-yl)	-	Spiritual one
Danyea (dan-yea)	-	Feelings of hope
Darcenia (dar-ceni-ah)	-	Loyal to God
DaShelle (dah-shell)	-	Peace
Daunea (dah-nea)	-	Follow the glory
Daveigh (dah-vay)	-	Born to worship God
Davie' (dah-vae)	-	Love in action
Davia (dah-v-ah)	-	Patience
Dawana (dah-wa-nah)	-	Gods glory
Dawnita (dah-nee-tah)	-	One who is blessed
Dawndra (don-dra)	-	Entering into glory
Dedra (dee-dra)	-	To prosper
Deana (de-an-ah)	-	One who believes
Deanika (dean-e-kah)	-	Savior
Dearria (dee-are-e-ah)	-	Born of God
De Arria (dee-ah-ree-ah)	-	Joyous Heart
Deasha (D-shay)	-	Entering God's goodness
Debonila (deb-on-ilah)	-	Wise one
Deborah (deh-bor-ah)	-	Creator with God
D'Juana (d-wanna)	-	Acting on faith
Deaja (day-jah)	-	Following my purpose
De'jah (day-jah)	-	Following the way of love
Deka (d-kah)	-	Holding on to God
Dekia (deck-e-ah)	-	One who is determined
Demekia (deh-me-kee-ah)	-	Touching God
Demetreus (de-me-tree-us)	-	Giving honor and glory
Demetria (de-me-tree-ah)	-	Deliverer
Deni (den-aye)	-	Tasteful one
Denusha (den-oo-sha)	-	Lovely one
Depirria (de-pir-ria)	-	God lives within

Derika (deh-ree-kah)	-	Messenger
De' sha (day-sha)	-	Truly good
Deshana (de-shanna)	-	Glorious one
Deshelle (desh-ell)	-	One who is destined
Devern (d-vern)	-	Finding truth in God
Deyanna (d-yanna)	-	The nature of God
Dion (d-yon)	-	Bright one
Dirona (dir-on-ah)	-	True enlightenment
Diva (de-vah)	-	Absolute trust
Dominique (dom-mih-neek)	-	unique
Dommonique (dom-mo-neek)	-	Finding God's way
Doniquandria (doni-quan-dria)	-	Sun Goddess
Doretha (dor-e-tha)	-	Sincere
Dorthia (dor-e-thee-ah)	-	Energetic
Drion (dree-on)	-	To love God more
Dwanna (d-wanna)	-	Living in spirit

E

Ebonie (eb-on-nee)	-	Good steward
Edith (e-dith)	-	Heart warming
Ednah (ed-nah)	-	Following God's light
Elmeka (el-me-kah)	-	Following good things
Enid (e-nid)	-	To follow God
Edwena (ed-wee-nah)	-	Wealthy
Eldyne (el-deen)	-	Being God's voice
Electra (e-lec-tra)	-	Brilliant light
Elita (eh-lee-tah)	-	leader
Elouise (eh-loo-ees)	-	One who honors God
Emelia (eh-me-lee-ah)	-	Creative
Enid (e-nid)	-	One who follows Christ
Enita (eh-nee-tah)	-	Ambitious one
Enola (e-no-lah)	-	All goodness
Eona (e-o-nah)	-	God's companion
Erickah (eh-re-kah)	-	Independent one

Erkard (er-kard)	-	Following God's works
Errista (err-is-tah)	-	Strength
Esonya (e-son-ya)	-	Paradise
Essence (es-ence)	-	Beginning of life
Estasha (es-tay-sha)	-	Friendly one
Euniquea (u-ne-que-ah)	-	Feeling God's love
Eve Shudann (eve-shu-dahn)	-	To find peace
Excentra (ex-cen-tra)	-	Exciting

F

Faith (fay-th)	-	Faithful
Fallon (fa-lon)	-	A gift from God
Faiza (fay-zia)	-	Devoted one
Falana (fah-lah-nah)	-	Power of God
Falza (fal-zah)	-	One who is happy
Fandola (fan-doe-lah)	-	One who dominates
Fashawn (fah-shon)	-	God mind
Fashola (fah-sho-lah)	-	Abundant joy
Fatima (fah-tee-mah)	-	Miracle worker
Felencia (feh-len-cia)	-	imagination
Felicia (feh-lee-cia)	-	Strong feelings
Felina (feh-lee-nah)	-	Small one
Felisa (feh-lee-sah)	-	Great and wonderful
Felitta (feh-lee-tah)	-	Grace and love
Feria (feh-rea)	-	Flower child
Fiola (fe-o-lah)	-	Beloved
Fiana (fe-ah-nah)	-	Little rose
Florhonda (flo-ron-dah)	-	To honor God's will
Floritta (flor-ee-tah)	-	Finding grace within
Fontessa (fon-tess-ah)	-	Abundant life
Funa (foo-nah)	-	Melodious
Funica (foo-ni-kah)	-	Gods love
Fushinia (foo-shih-nee-ah)	-	Abounding grace

G

Gabrielle (gab-ree-el)	-	Voice of God
Gale (gay-l)	-	Pretty and smart
Genesis (gen-eh-sis)	-	The beginning of life
Genice (gen-eese)	-	Kind spirit
Gensella (gen-sella)	-	Choosing the right path.
Gestella (ges-tella)	-	Protective
Geta (gee-tah)	-	Gentle
Giacentia (gee-ah-cen-tee-ah)	-	Mother of light
Giana (g-ana)	-	New dawn
Gina (g-nah)	-	Humble one
Giovonna (geo-vahn-ah)	-	God is gracious
Gisele (gis-el)	-	Showing God's favor
Gistasha (gis-tah-sha)	-	To know light
Glori (glor-ree)	-	Coming to God in peace
Gloristine (glor-is-teen)	-	True light of God
Glover (glo-ver)	-	Light of venus
Glynnis (glyn-is)	-	Gods perfection
Gonetha (gon-e-tha)	-	One presence

H

Hadassah (ha-dah-sah)	-	Giving to God's people
Hafeezah (ha-fee-sah)	-	Coming to God in prayer
Hakesha (ha-kee-sha)	-	Healing spirit
Halie (hal-ee)	-	Triumphant
Halona (hal-o-nah)	-	Ray of light
Harmoni (har-mo-nee)	-	One who sings
Hashawn (ha-shon)	-	Healer of hearts
Hasana (ha-sah-nah)	-	High spirit
Hattie (hat-ee)	-	Hopeful
Heather (heh-ther)	-	Flower
Hermetria (her-mee-tree-ah)	-	Shining star
Hineah (hih-nee-ah)	-	God knows

Hillory (hil-ory)	-	Stately
Hisanna (his-ah-nah)	-	Unlimited good
Honesty (on-es-tee)	-	Giving God glory
Hortessa (hor-tes-ah)	-	Coming back to God
Hoshana (ho-sonna)	-	Loving presence

I

Icelyn (ice-lyn)	-	Happiness & peace
Icheryl (ih-cheryl)	-	One who shares
Ilond (I-lond)	-	God's precious gift
Illiah (il-lee-ah)	-	To obey God
Imelia (e-me-le-ah)	-	One who is positive
Imunique (I'm-unique)	-	Radiant Sunshine
Inisha (ih-nih-sha)	-	Determined
Innisa (ih-nis-ah)	-	Lord of the land
Isha (e-sha)	-	God's kingdom come
Ishambre (ish-sham-bray)	-	Guardian angel
Ishante (ish-on-tay)	-	Gods goodness
Ishina (ish-she-nah)	-	My heart
Ishmetta (ish-metta)	-	Mountain of love
Ishuna (ish-uh-nah)	-	Hope of glory
Issi (is-ee)	-	Sunshine
Isys (is-ees)	-	Heavenly favorite
Iyania (e-yon-e-ah)	-	One who inspires
Iyanna (e-yon-nah)	-	God's favorite child

J

Ja (jah)	-	God's one and only
JaBria (jah-bre-ah)	-	One who brings peace
Jacqueline (jah-quel-lyn)	-	Fighter
Jada (jay-dah)	-	Wealth and splendor
Jade (jay-d)	-	Following Christ
Jael (jay-el)	-	Precious stone.

Jakaya (jah-ky-ah)	-	Feelings of greatness
Jakayla (jah-kay-lah)	-	Happy and loving
Jakkita (jah-kee-tah)	-	High consciousness
Jalonda (jah-lon-dah)	-	Holding God's peace
Jamani (jah-mon-nee)	-	Standing strong
Jameilah (jah-mee-lah)	-	Instructor
Jameze (jah-meez)	-	Joining hands with God
Jami (jay-me)	-	God's temple
Jana (jay-nah)	-	Giving to God
Janai (jah-nye)	-	God's presence
Janeeka (jon-e-kah)	-	Sheild of faith
Janiya (jah-nee-yah)	-	Favoring God
Janelle (jah-neel)	-	Following God's order
Janessa (jah-ness-ah)	-	A new life
Janetta (jon-etta)	-	To rejoice
Jania (jon-ne-ah)	-	One who is saved
Janice (jan-is)	-	One who provides
Janissa (jan-iss-ah)	-	One love
Janita (jan-ee-tah)	-	Believing God
Jannel (jon-el)	-	Bright shining star
Janya (jan-e-ah)	-	To see Gods will
Jaquetta (jah-quet-tah)	-	All wisdom
Jaquitta (jah-quitt-ah)	-	Following spirits lead
Jaslene (jaz-leen)	-	Finding grace in God.
Jasmin (jaz-min)	-	Gods flower
Jateria (jah-terry-ah)	-	Joining in love
JaTya (jah-tye-ah)	-	Finding Gods spirit.
Jayla (jay-lah)	-	Growing in God's love
Jaynesha (jay-nee-sha)	-	Needing God's presence
Jean (jeen)	-	Guided by God
Jecina (jeh-see-nah)	-	spiritually centered
Jene' (jeh-nay)	-	Tribute to God
Jenkesha (jen-kee-sha)	-	Prophet
Jennica (jen-e-kah)	-	Gods messenger

Jennifur (jen-ne-fur)	-	To feel great
Jenyla (jen-eye-lah)	-	Having access to God
Jericka (jeh-rick-ah)	-	To praise God
Jessette (jeh-set)	-	Power within
Jiana (jee-ana)	-	Streams of goodness
Jiaya (jy-yah)	-	Always giving thanks
Jimalita (jim-ah-lee-tah)	-	To work in love
Joan (joe-n)	-	Protected by God
JoAngela (joe-angela)	-	Word of faith
Joayn (jo-an)	-	Having faith in yourself
Johna' (jon-a)	-	To have hope
Johnasia (john-asia)	-	Meaningful life
Joi (joy)	-	Glowing in God's presence
Jolisha (joe-lee-sha)	-	Honoring God's work
Jonair (joe-nair)	-	To feel safe
Jonda (jon-dah)	-	Spirit of peace
Jonell (jon-el)	-	Feelings of warmth
Jonikka (jon-e-kah)	-	To finish first
Jordan (jor-dan)	-	Strength of Christ
JoVon (joe-vahn)	-	Hungry for life
Jovita (joe-vee-tah)	-	Following goodness
Joyce (joy-s)	-	Measure of faith
Joyetta (joe-vet-ah)	-	Greatness
Juannessa (won-ness-ah)	-	Building Strength
Jumoke (ju-moe-kay)	-	Truth teacher
Juneka (ju-nee-kah)	-	Light of nations
Jutesia (ju-tee-see-ah)	-	Wonder of life
Juwan (Ju-won)	-	Goodness and truth
Jykayla (Jih-kay-lah)	-	Strong voice

K

Kacia (kay-see-ah)	-	Wonderful one
Kai (kay)	-	Loveable
Kalah (kay-lah)	-	Vibration of perfection

Kalayah (kah-lay-ah)	-	To grow in understanding
Kalea (kah-lee-ah)	-	To glory in God
Kaleka (kah-lee-kah)	-	Born in goodness
Kalere (kah-leer-ree)	-	A sacred Rose
Kameel (kah-meal)	-	Praise and honor
Kametra (kah-me-tra)	-	Holy one of God
Kamica (kah-me-kah)	-	Following Gods guidance
Kamico (kah-me-ko)	-	Creative imagination
Kamike' (kah-me-kay)	-	Seeing God's truth
Kamilah (kah-me-lah)	-	Very dear to God
Kanika (kah-nee-kah)	-	To receive God's blessings
Kanilah (kah-nee-lah)	-	Wonder of love
Kara (kah-rah)	-	Halo of light
Karima (Kah-ree-mah)	-	Loving you
Karlotta (car-lot-ah)	-	Divine purpose
Kamaria (kah-mar-e-ah)	-	Truth and power
Karnetta (car-net-tah)	-	Merciful one
Kathia (kah-thee-ah)	-	To send love
Katrina (kah-trina)	-	God protects
Kayla (kay-lah)	-	Peace of God
Kawana (kah-wanna)	-	Powerful spirit
Kawanis (kah-wannis)	-	One with nature
Kawanya (kah-wan-yah)	-	God's faithful servant
Kecia (keh-see-ah)	-	Finishing God's work
Keela (kee-lah)	-	Growing in goodness
Keenyette (keen-yet)	-	Counselor
Keesha (key-sha)	-	Sparkling light
Keitha (kee-tha)	-	Spirit of life
Kela (kee-lah)	-	Mastering faith
Keleshia (kee-leh-shia)	-	True beauty
Kellita (kel-lit-ah)	-	True faith
Kelly (kel-lee)	-	Having faith
Kelsy (kel-see)	-	To follow God's will
Kemi (keh-me)	-	Guidance

Kemia (keh-me-ah)	-	Growing in God
Kemmya (keh-my-ah)	-	Finding spirit
Kencella (ken-cel-ah)	-	One who is healthy
Kendesea (ken-des-e-ah)	-	Lord of love
Kendra (ken-dra)	-	God is all
Kenita (ken-e-tah)	-	Light
Keniya (ken-i-yah)	-	Choosing right thoughts
Keona (kee-o-nah)	-	Forceful power
Kerryann (kerry-ann)	-	Moving in God
Keyota (key-o-tah)	-	God's loving grace
Keri (kerry)	-	Thoughtful
Kenya (ken-yah)	-	Personality of God
Kenyada (ken-ya-dah)	-	Finding peace within
Kesa (key-sah)	-	moving in spirit
Keyosha (key-o-sha)	-	Following God's law
Keyshia (key-she-ah)	-	Following my word
Khadejah (kah-dee-jah)	-	God spirit
Khalilah (kah-lee-lah)	-	Youthful spirit
Khayla (kay-lah)	-	Peace of God
Khonilah (kon-nih-lah)	-	Affectionate
Khristilyn (chris-tih-lyn)	-	Following the Lords prayer
Kiaesha (ky-e-sha)	-	To dwell upon God
Kiamethia (key-ah-meth-iah)	-	To choose God
Kiawanna (key-ah-wanna)	-	To win in life
Kierne (keer-nee)	-	Order
Kijuan (key-won)	-	Living for Christ
Kimesha (kim-esha)	-	Pure spirit
Kimethia (kim-e-thia)	-	Loving God
Kiosha (key-o-sha)	-	Feeling God's goodness
Kirsten (keer-sten)	-	The anointed one
Kikanza (key-kon-zah)	-	Gods wealth
Kilwon (kil-won)	-	Grace
Kimberly (kim-ber-lee)	-	Truth & Wisdom
Kimisean (kimi-shon)	-	God gives life

Kishan (key-shon)	-	To feel God's joy
Kori (korry)	-	Warm hearted
Kotasha (ko-tash-ah)	-	Strong in God
Komainee (ko-mahn-nee)	-	Strong leader
Kowanda (ko-wanda)	-	Accepted in God
Kryshelle (krih-shell)	-	Needing Gods hand
Krysten (chris-ten)	-	Forming good thoughts
Krystle (kris-tl)	-	Showing God love
Kure (cure)	-	Kind hearted
Kwanda (k-wanda)	-	Wisdom and truth
Kyera (ky-err-ah)	-	I am power
Kyla (ky-lah)	-	Noble
Kylie (ky-lee)	-	To keep God's promises
Kyrra (ky-rah)	-	Born pretty

L

LaBraya (lah-bray-yah)	-	God blessed
LaCheryl (lah-cheh-ryl)	-	Blessings of truth
Lacinda (lah-cin-dah)	-	Cheerful one
Ladina (lah-deena)	-	A joy to behold
Ladonna (lah-donna)	-	Truth
Lakeia (lah-kee-ah)	-	Truly sent by God
Lakeisel (lah-kee-sell)	-	The life force of God
Lakeisha (lah-kee-sha)	-	Obedient
LaKetha (lah-kee-tha)	-	Adding light to love
Lakeysha (lah-kee-sha)	-	Moving into God's goodness
Lakieta (lah-kee-tah)	-	Valuable
Lakita (lah-kee-tah)	-	Strong and mighty
Lakwonda (lah-kwon-dah)	-	The giver of love
Lalisha (lah-lee-sha)	-	The gift of life
LaMesha (lah-mee-sha)	-	Gods love
Lamika (lah-mee-kah)	-	To share God's word
Lamonica (lah-mon-ih-kah)	-	The intellectual
Lamonte (lah-mon-tay)	-	Great wealth

La Paris (lah-paris)	-	Giving God love
Laquanya (lah-quon-yah)	-	To see God's light
Laquina (lah-quin-ah)	-	Lady of love
Laquisa (lah-kee-sah)	-	God within
LaQuisha (lah-key-sha)	-	Moving forward
Laquita (lah-key-tah)	-	The will to love
LaShanda (lah-shon-dah)	-	The light of God
Lashawn (lah-shon)	-	Victorious
LaShwen (lah-shwen)	-	Glorious child of God
Lataetka (lah-tah-eat-kah)	-	Gallant & strong
Latangya (lah-ton-yah)	-	To glorify the father
Latanya (la-ton-yah)	-	The rock of salvation
Latasha (lah-tah-sha)	-	Gentle touch
LaTesha (lah-tee-sha)	-	Winning heart
Latifah (la-tee-fah)	-	The faithful one
Latisha (lah-tee-sha)	-	The wonder of God
Latoya (la-toy-yah)	-	Girl baby
LaTrina (la-tree-nah)	-	Powerful servant
Latrise (la-tree-s)	-	Strong foundation
LaTrisha (lah-trish-ah)	-	The trinity
Latika (lah-tee-kah)	-	One who is glorious
Latisha (lah-tih-sha)	-	Showering love
Lattica (la-tih-kah)	-	Love of God
Laurette (lau-ret)	-	Needing Gods joy
Lauri (lau-ree)	-	Messenger of peace
Lavantae (lah-von-tay)	-	Glorious in mercy
Lavine (lah-vine)	-	To fast and pray
Lavonne (lah-von-e)	-	One with power
Layla (lay-lah)	-	Holding Gods presence
Layondra (lah-yon-drah)	-	To love peace
Laysha (lay-sha)	-	Soothing spirit
Lazheta (lay-zet-ah)	-	Coming from the universe
Learetha (lee-ah-re-tha)	-	True spirit
Leatrice (lee-ah-treece)	-	Full of great works

LeCherie (lay-cher-e)	-	My love
LeCherrone (lay-cher-rone)	-	My flower
Lentha (len-tha)	-	To provide joy
Lesha (lee-sha)	-	God abides within
Le'stacia (leh-stay-see-ah)	-	Following wisdom
Levonne (lay-von)	-	To feel good
Lina (lee-nah)	-	One with truth
Linda (lin-dah)	-	Beautiful
Liah (lee-ah)	-	Golden girl
Linnea (lin-e-ah)	-	Loving God more
Li'Yana (lee-yan-ah)	-	God's shining star
Lizette (liz-ett)	-	Knowing God's goodness
Lolita (low-lee-tah)	-	One who comforts
Lonetta (lon-eh-tah)	-	God's glory
Lorah (lor-ah)	-	To give more
Lorea (lor-e-ah)	-	Strong in faith
Lorelei (lor-e-lie)	-	Victorious spirit
Lorenity (lor-en-ih-te)	-	Walking in faith
Loretha (lor-e-tha)	-	Born of love
Loriel (lor-e-el)	-	Bright one
Loticia (low-tih-sha)	-	All is well
Louise (loo-e-s)	-	Giving nature
Loukisha (loo-kee-sha)	-	Following God's ways
Lourdes (lord-es)	-	To feel special
Lourisha (loo-rih-sah)	-	God of love
Lucretia (loo-cree-sha)	-	Overflowing love
Lula (loo-lah)	-	Loving God's word
Luna (loo-nah)	-	To be filled with light
Lynwellyn (lyn-well-in)	-	Giving thanks to God

M

Machandra (mah-chon dra)	-	Finding grace and peace
Madara (mah-dare-ah)	-	God's love
Mandisa (man-dis-ah)	-	Pointing to Christ

Maia (my-ah)	-	To focus on love
Makia (mah-kee-ah)	-	Lord of light
Makiya (mah-key-ah)	-	To know God's goodness
Makini (mah-kee-nee)	-	Precious child of God
Maleeka (mah-lee-kah)	-	All that God is
Malia (mah-lee-ah)	-	Spirited
Malika (mah-lee-kah)	-	Pure consciousness
Malinda (mah-lin-dah)	-	Beautiful one
Marcella (mar-sel-lah)	-	Heir of God
Maranda (mah-ran-dah)	-	Coming to God in truth
Marcheta (mar-cheh-tah)	-	A ray of sunshine
Marcia (mar-see-ah)	-	Soundness
Marell (mar-el)	-	Togetherness
Marhanda (mar-hand-ah)	-	Honoring God's call
Marinesha (marin-e-sha)	-	Harmony
Marketa (mar-kee-tah)	-	Peace & blessings
Markeyea (mar-key-ah)	-	Spirit of liberty
Markia (mar-kee-ah)	-	Full of blessings
Marina (mar-e-nah)	-	Tranquil
Marissa (mar-is-ah)	-	Forgiving love
Marita (mar-e-tah)	-	Standing on faith
Marrita (mar-rita)	-	Kingdom blessings
Martine (mar-teen)	-	Shielded by faith
Marquetta (mar-ket-ah)	-	One who is strong
Marquita (mar-qui-tah)	-	Gods sunshine
Maryna (mar-e-nah)	-	To glorify the Lord
Marshandra (mar-shon-drah)	-	United in love
Marshaun (mar-shon)	-	Calling forth goodness
Marvel (mar-vel)	-	Growing close to God
Mashanti (mah-shon-tee)	-	God is in charge
Mawakana (mah-wah-kon-nah)	-	Yielding to Gods will
Maya (my-ah)	-	Song of love
Mayetta (my-etta)	-	Truth of being
Meah (me-ah)	-	Giving true love

Mellani (mel-on-nee)	-	The temple of God
Mena (me-nah)	-	My new life
Mercedes (mer-say-dees)	-	God's special one
Mia (me-ah)	-	My strength
Miansha (me-on-sha)	-	God centered
Micah (my-cah)	-	Reaching new heights
Michelle (mih-shell)	-	Child of God
Micherrie (mih-sherry)	-	Feelings of peace
Michiyo (mih-chy-o)	-	Beautiful, intelligent, forever
Mika (me-kah)	-	Prosperous and abundant
Mikalah (mih-kay-lah)	-	Wonderful life
Milan (mih-lon)	-	Tuning in to love
Milinda (mih-lin-dah)	-	One with high vision
Millisent (mil-is-cent)	-	Giving of my love
Minique (min-eek)	-	To offer love
Mira (my-rah)	-	One of courage
Mishay (mih-shay)	-	My gift
Moiya (mo-e-yah)	-	To know God's nature
Monika (mon-ih-kah)	-	Spark of divinity
Moveda (mo-ve-dah)	-	Choosing God's love
Muneen (mun-een)	-	Finding grace through love
Musette (mu-sette)	-	Feeling loved
Myesha (my-e-sha)	-	Mercy and truth
Myrtice (mir-tee-s)	-	Beautiful spirit
Myshaun (my-shon)	-	Feeling cherished

N

Nadia (nah-dee-ah)	-	Leaning toward God
Nadine (nay-deen)	-	Mighty one
Nadirah (nah-deer-ah)	-	Holding onto peace
Nadra (nah-dra)	-	Truth prevails
Naeemah (ny-ema)	-	Crowning glory
Nafeesa (na-fee-sah)	-	I am blessed
Nahla (nah-lah)	-	Seeing Gods light

Naiya (na-e-yah)	-	Yielding to love
Najah (nah-jah)	-	Born to love
Nakia (nah-key-ah)	-	Born in love
Nakita (nah-key-tah)	-	Blessed love
Nala (nah-lah)	-	Lioness
Nani (nah-nee)	-	Feeling special
Naomi (nay-o-me)	-	I turn within
Naquanda (nah-kwon-dah)	-	Giving grace to God
Nara (nah-rah)	-	To guide and direct
Nariah (nah-rye-ah)	-	In God's spirit
Narissa (nah-rissa)	-	Mighty love
Narcissa (nar-sis-ah)	-	Going to God in prayer
Nasheka (nah-she-kah)	-	Strengthened by love
Natalia (nah-tali-ah)	-	Great Communicator
Natalie (nat-ah-lee)	-	Songstress
Natasha (nah-tah-sha)	-	Delightful
Natiesha (nah-tee-sha)	-	Bonding with God
Natine (nah-teen)	-	Precious
Natisha (nah-tih-sha)	-	Covered in grace
Nawell (nah-well)	-	To give unto God
Nazaria (nah-zah-ree-ah)	-	Listening for Gods word
Nechandra (neh-chon-dra)	-	Winning in Christ
Neesha (nee-sha)	-	Gift of love
Nekeasia (neh-kee-see-ah)	-	Peaceful nature
Netanya (neh-ton-ya)	-	Born of love
Nichelle (nih-shell)	-	Mothers joy
Nicholette (nih-ko-let)	-	Gift from God
Nicole (nih-cole)	-	Spirit child
Nikia (nih-kee-ah)	-	The will of God
Nikita (nih-kee-tah)	-	Heavenly glow
Nikyta (nih-kee-tah)	-	Shower of faith
Nilah (ny-lah)	-	Love flows
Nile (ny-l)	-	Following Gods goodness
Nina (ne-nah)	-	Rich in love

Nisha (nih-sha)	-	Everywhere present
Nitara (nih-tah-rah)	-	Symbol of healing
Nitza (nit-zah)	-	Honoring God through love
Niya (ny-yah)	-	Sweet blossom
Norell (nor-el)	-	Fighting spirit
Noriel (nor-e-el)	-	Labor of love
Nushaun (nu-shon)	-	Dainty
Novella (no-vella)	-	Little one
Nykeria (nih-kerri-ah)	-	Truth and beauty

O

Octavia (oc-tav-e-ah)	-	Pillar of strength
Odia (o-de-ah)	-	Family centered
Olamide' (o-lah-me-day)	-	My joy has come
Oluwakemi (o-lu-wa-keh-me)	-	God is my guidance
Omalia (o-mah-lee-ah)	-	God leads me
Omisha (o-mee-sha)	-	Goodness & beauty
Oprah (o-prah)	-	Angel of God
Oquisha (o-kee-sha)	-	Love inspired
Oriana (or-e-ana)	-	Friend to all
Orisha (or-ish-ah)	-	Gleaming
Orita (or-e-tah)	-	Made in love
Orelon (or-lon)	-	Seeing Gods beauty
Ormana (or-mah-nah)	-	Kindhearted
Ortabia (or-tah-be-ah)	-	Beneath the wind
Ortabria (or-tah-bre-ah)	-	Timeless beauty
Osani (o-sah-nee)	-	Sound of nature
Ozeheta (oz-etta)	-	Happy child
Ozeon (o-zee-on)	-	Channel for God

P

Paris (paa-ris)	-	Believing inGod
Page (pa-g)	-	God's nature

Pamela (pam-eh-lah)	-	Precious child
Paradise (paa-rah-dice)	-	Holding onto glory
Patia (pah-te-ah)	-	Crown of faith
Patra (pay-tra)	-	To glorify God
Patricia (pat-rih-sha)	-	Complete faith
Paulette (paul-ette)	-	Gods great joy
Pernita (per-nee-tah)	-	Calling out to God
Persia (per-sha)	-	Gift of God
Petice (peh-teese)	-	Wholeness
Petula (peh-tu-lah)	-	Goddess of love
Peyton (pay-ton)	-	God'precious child
Phoebie (fee-bee)	-	Center of love
Pheona (fee-o-nah)	-	Gods perfect law
Pinetta (pin-etta)	-	God never fails
Pinette (pin-ette)	-	Gods help
Polietta (poly-etta)	-	Under God's will
Preclonia (pre-clo-nia)	-	Creative intellegence
Preon (pre-on)	-	Glorifying God
Pricella (pri-cella)	-	Solid rock
Princella (prin-cella)	-	God hears me
Prinstella (prin-stella)	-	God speed
Pristine (pris-tine)	-	Honorable one

Q

Qiani (qee-ah-nee)	-	Finding faith in God
Quanisha (quon-ih-sha)	-	To have love for God
Quantisha (quon-tih-sha)	-	Gods perfect will
Quantiyanna (quon-tee-ana)	-	Established in love
Quateaka (quah-tee-kah)	-	True goodness
Queeta (quee-tah)	-	Filled with Gods spirit
Quenna (quen-nah)	-	Heavens queen
Quentana (quen-tana)	-	Surrounded by God
Quertha (qu-err-tha)	-	Gods diving plan
Quiana (qee-ana)	-	Turn to God

Quillie (quih-lee)	-	Feeling safe in God
Quinesha (quin-e-sha)	-	Everlasting arms
Quinn (quin)	-	To love all
Quinteta (quin-teh-tah)	-	Faith of God
Quishera (qee-sheh-rah)	-	God's with you
Quita (quee-tah)	-	Gods shining light
Quronica (q-ron-ih-kah)	-	Finding love
Quwanyu (q-won-u)	-	Answering God's will

R

Rachisha (rah-she-sha)	-	To find faith
Raenee (ray-nee)	-	Giving strength
Rafeequllah (rah-fee-qu-lah)	-	To make whole
Rafica (rah-fee-kah)	-	Lean on God
Rahema (rah-he-mah)	-	Life, Love & wisdom
Rakeisha (rah-kee-sha)	-	Princess of God
Rakisha (rah-kee-sha)	-	Total love
Ralonda (rah-lon-dah)	-	Couteous
Ramiele (ray-me-el)	-	Honest and true
Ramile (rah-meel)	-	Filled with light
Ramiyah (rah-me-yah)	-	Entering love
Rasanee (rah-sah-nee)	-	Feel the power
Rasha (rah-sha)	-	Warm and loving
Rasheeda (rah-she-dah)	-	Wisdom and glory
Rashida (rah-she-dah)	-	Strong mountain
Raqkeha (rah-kee-ha)	-	Strong rock of hope
Raquita (rah-qui-tah)	-	Positive and faith filled
Ratasha (rah-tah-sha)	-	Finding grace
Ravin (ray-vin)	-	Strong messenger
Rayven (ray-ven)	-	Going with God
Reah (ree-ah)	-	God is merciful
Rebekah (reh-bee-kah)	-	Highly blessed
Reeshemah (ray-she-mah)	-	Growing in spirit
Regina (reh-gee-nah)	-	Positive mind

Rehema (reh-he-mah)	-	Lasting love
Relly (rel-lee)	-	Staying true to God
Renata (ren-ah-tah)	-	Loving one
Renee (re-nay)	-	Glory of God
Renetta (re-netta)	-	Amazing joy
Reshon (re-shon)	-	Unlimited intelligence
Retrice (reh-treece)	-	Grounded in spirit
Richelle (rih-shell)	-	Eternal life
Reshon (reh-shon)	-	Coming to life
Richlynne (rich-lyn)	-	Opening up to wisdom
Ricke (rih-kee)	-	God property
Rickia (rih-kee-ah)	-	Sweet child
Rika (ree-kah)	-	Sister of love
Ritiea (rih-tee-ah)	-	Stand in faith
Robin (rob-in)	-	Musical
Roncita (ron-see-tah)	-	In Gods hands
Roneaka (ron-e-kah)	-	Trusting in God
Rosemond (rose-mond)	-	Peacefulness
Roshanna (ro-sha-nah)	-	Highest love
Rouena (roo-e-nah)	-	Goodness, mercy, love
Rozetta (rose-etta)	-	Love flower
Rukiya (roo-key-ah)	-	Mother of mercy

S

Saadaqah (sah-dah-quah)	-	Strength in God
Sabra (say-brah)	-	Sweet patience
Sabria (say-bree-ah)	-	Enduring love
Sabrina (sah-bree-nah)	-	Patient love
Sakina (sah-kee-nah)	-	Believing in God
Salon (sah-lon)	-	Thankful for life
Salonge (sah-lon-g)	-	Good flows to me
Salvation (sal-vay-shun)	-	God's purpose
Samaria (sah-mah-ree-ah)	-	Glory in peace
Samena (sah-me-nah)	-	Sweet spirit

Samerra (sah-meh-rah)	-	Returning to love
Sanaa (san-ah)	-	Moving with wisdom
Sandra (sand-rah)	-	Energy of God
Saneka (sah-nee-kah)	-	Giving God the glory
Sanoplia (san-o-plee-ah)	-	Enlightened
Santita (san-tee-tah)	-	Feeling God's wisdom
Saundrell (sawn-drell)	-	Coming into goodness
Saxanie (sax-an-nee)	-	uncommon love
Screda (scree-dah)	-	God's joy within
Scymaka (skee-mah-kah)	-	glorify the lord
Seandra (shon-drah)	-	To follow God's word
Sekaya (seh-kay-ah)	-	Giving back to God
Selicia (she-lee-see-ah)	-	Feelings of joy
Selitta (seh-lit-ah)	-	Thou art worthy
Selma (sel-mah)	-	Love returns
Sema (see-mah)	-	Being true to God
Sena (see-nah)	-	Finding God's truth
Serenity (ser-ren-ih-te)	-	Abundant peace
Shae (shay)	-	To love life
Shaiya (shy-ah)	-	Messenger of God
Shakara (sha-kah-rah)	-	God's beauty
Shakira (sha-kir-ah)	-	Strong faith
Shakita (sha-kee-tah)	-	Choosing to love
Shalece (sha-lee-s)	-	To be sincere
Shaloma (sha-lo-mah)	-	Obedience
Shalonda (sha-lon-dah)	-	Fountain of youth
Shalondra (sha-lon-drah)	-	Ambitious
Shamakha (sha-mah-kah)	-	Joy and happiness
Shamara (sha-mah-rah)	-	Lovingly live life
Shameka (sha-me-kah)	-	Pure love
Shamekia (sha-me-kee-ah)	-	To finish with greatness
Shana (sha-nah)	-	Causing greatness
Shaneka (sha-nee-kah)	-	Moving forward with God
Shanethia (sha-nee-thee-ah)	-	Giving Gods glory

Shanick (shan-eek)	-	Showing God's goodness
Shanikra (sha-nee-kra)	-	Following God's truth
Shanta (shon-tah)	-	Perfect child
Shantal (shon-tall)	-	God's jewel
Shantae' (shon-tay)	-	Wonderful person
Shantee (shon-tee)	-	Angel of laughter
Shanteria (shon-teh-ree-ah)	-	Listening for God
Shantilata (shon-tih-lotta)	-	Having God's wisdom
Shantras (shon-tra-s)	-	True to God's word
Shaguandra (sha-guon-dra)	-	Finding peace with God
Shaquanda (sha-quon-dra)	-	Gods loving works
Shaquisha (sha-kee-sha)	-	Beautiful eagle
Shareece (shar-reece)	-	Seeing Gods goodness
Shari (shar-ree)	-	Making progress in God
Sharikka (sha-ree-kah)	-	Giving praise to God
Sharis (sha-ris)	-	Gentleness
Sharita (shar-e-tah)	-	Promising greatness
Sharnette (shar-net)	-	Following Christ's wisdom
Sharisse (shar-reece)	-	Under God's presence
Sharon (shaa-ron)	-	To feel pure
Shatica (sha-tee-kah)	-	Hearing God's spirit
Shatoya (sha-toy-ah)	-	Living by grace
Shauntae (shon-tay)	-	Filled with light
Shaunquetta (shon-queh-tah)	-	Thinking of God
Shavonne (sha-von)	-	Staying close to God
Shawanna (sha-wanna)	-	Special to God
Shawn (shon)	-	Thankful one
Shawnekia (shon-ee-kee-ah)	-	Proving God's word
Shaya (shay-ah)	-	Finding wisdom
Shayla (shay-lah)	-	Tuning into love
Shayoon (shay-oon)	-	Giving God the praise
Sheelan (she-lon)	-	Mountain flower
Shelly (shell-e)	-	Listening to God
Sherain (sher-rain)	-	Giving God's love

Sherea (sheh-ree-ah)	-	Foundation in God
Sherina (sher-e-nah)	-	To search for truth
Sherita (sheh-ree-tah)	-	Great inspiration
Sherlanda (sher-land-ah)	-	Following God
Shermika (sher-me-kah)	-	Lovely child
Sherran (sher-ran)	-	Finding God's purpose
Sherwin (sher-win)	-	Gentleness and goodness
Sheshanda (shay-shon-dah)	-	Finding wisdom in God
Shevon (sheh-von)	-	Woman of love
Sheyeen (sheh-yeen)	-	Wonderful counselor
Shianti (she-on-tee)	-	Carrying God within
Shirlee (shir-lee)	-	Peace and love
Shondis (shon-dis)	-	Attractive
Shontina (shon-tina)	-	Activating kindness
Shosharah (sho-sha-rah)	-	Cloud of joy
Shoundra (shon-dra)	-	God is good
Shyrone (shih-rone)	-	Peace be with me
Sidnie (sid-nee)	-	Giving love to God
Simena (see-men-nah)	-	Finding the father
Sitara (sih-tah-rah)	-	Holy one
Sondra (son-drah)	-	Happy in love
Sonia (so-nea)	-	Women of gold
Sonja (son-jah)	-	Understanding faith
Stacey (stay-cee)	-	Needing God's guidance
Stacie (stay-see)	-	Charm and grace
Stanicia (stan-e-see-ah)	-	To follow your heart
Stanlisha (stan-lee-sha)	-	Holding onto God's grace
Star (st-ah-r)	-	God Shining light
Starmayne (star-maine)	-	To inspire
Steffney (stef-nee)	-	God's shinning light
Stevanna (steh-von-ah)	-	Remember God's goodness
Sue Ellen (su-el-en)	-	Familiar spirit
Syleena (sih-lee-nah)	-	Glory to God
Sokya (so-kee-ah)	-	One with divine ideas

Syesha (sy-ee-sha)	-	Prosperity and love
Symone (sih-mone)	-	God cares
Synai (sih-nye)	-	Joy and abundance
Syrketha (sir-kee-tha)	-	Winning in God

T

Tabrici (tab-ree-ce)	-	Filled with love
Tachia (tah-chee-nah)	-	Following after God
Taffi (taa-fee)	-	Gods strength
Tahappiness (tah-happy-ness)	-	God's goodness
Takari (tah-car-e)	-	Always sincere
Takayla (tah-kay-lah)	-	Centered in spirit
TaKelia (tah-kee-lee-ah)	-	Mothers pearl
Takia (tah-kee-ah)	-	Entering peace
Takisha (tah-kee-sha)	-	To move with God
Talia (tal-e-ah)	-	Golden child
Talica (tah-lee-kah)	-	God is within
Talisa (tah-lee-sah)	-	I believe
Talonda (tah-lon-dah)	-	Miracle of love
Tamara (tah-mah-rah)	-	One with spirit
Tamecia (tah-me-see-ah)	-	Working in God
Tamia (tah-me-ah)	-	Love and laughter
Tamika (tah-me-kah)	-	To hear wisdom
Tamico (tah-me-ko)	-	Full of grace
Tamla (tam-lah)	-	Holding on to truth
Tamlyn (tam-lyn)	-	Faith keeper
Tamna (tam-nah)	-	Giving truth and life
Tammesa (tam-e-sah)	-	God's great joy
Tandrea (tan-dree-ah)	-	Sister of mercy
Tanesha (tan-e-sha)	-	One with a Good heart
Tanganyika (tan-yan-nee-kah)	-	Trinity of being
Tania (tan-e-ah)	-	To spread love
Tanika (tan-ee-kah)	-	Feeling God's presence
Tanji (tan-jee)	-	Full of hope

Tannillia (tan-nil-e-ah)	-	Born of light
Taquida (tah-kee-dah)	-	To find goodness
Tara (tah-rah)	-	I behold Christ
Taraji (tah-rah-gee)	-	Great character
Taranesha (tah-ran-e-sha)	-	Grounded in faith
Taryn (tare-rin)	-	Sweet soul
Tasha (tah-sha)	-	Luminous
Tasjknik (tasj-nick)	-	Forever pleasing God
Tashawn (tah-shon)	-	Healing light
Tashona (tah-shon-ah)	-	Prosperous
Tassandra (tah-son-dra)	-	Feeling blessed
Taveina (tah-ven-e-ah)	-	To Follow truth
Tawan (tah-won)	-	Glowing in spirit
Tawanna (tah-wanna)	-	Witness for God
Tazonda (tah-zon-dah)	-	Peace and glory
Teaunda (tee-un-dah)	-	To find goodness
Teco (tee-ko)	-	Power to create
Teiana (t-an-nah)	-	Loving life
Tekaila (teh-ky-lah)	-	One with grace
Telma (tel-mah)	-	Mighty spirit
Tennessa (ten-nes-sah)	-	Peace be with you
Terique (tear-reek)	-	Knowing truth and spirit
Teriwanna (ter-e-wan-ah)	-	Covered in love
Terkela (ter-kee-lah)	-	Gift from above
Terrica (ter-e-kah)	-	Receiving God's healing
Tesa (teh-sah)	-	Having God's love
Thandiwe (ton-d-way)	-	Honor and grace
Thea (thee-ah)	-	Strong courage
Theda (thee-dah)	-	Be still
Theosha (thee-o-sha)	-	Faith & love
Tia (t-ah)	-	A true blessing
Tianna (t-an-ah)	-	Finding faith
Tichandra (tih-shon-dra)	-	Connected to power
Tichina (tih-she-nah)	-	Born for greatness

Tierney (tear-nee)	-	Unselfish love
Tierra (t-err-ah)	-	God's law fulfilled
Tiffany (tif-ah-nee)	-	Precious jewel
Tiffini (tif-fin-e)	-	To work for God
Timeshia (tih-me-she-ah)	-	Perfect harvest
Tina (t-nah)	-	One who is bright
T'keyah (t'key-ah)	-	Full of mercy
Toiya (toy-ah)	-	God's joy
Tomaria (toe-mah-re-ah)	-	Glad spirit
Tomeka (toe-me-kah)	-	Right action
Tondra (ton-drah)	-	God's cup of love
Tonette (tone-et)	-	Finding God's will
Tonia (tone-e-ah)	-	Answering God's call
Tonica (tone-ih-kah)	-	To model God
Toniqua (tone-e-quah)	-	I am
Tosha (tosh-ah)	-	Abide in the presence
Toshca (toe-she-kah)	-	Finding the father
Tosi (toss-e)	-	Walk in victory
Toyana (toy-ana)	-	Loving child
Toyin (toy-in)	-	Goodness & mercy
Tracy (tray-see)	-	Richly blessed
Tranesha (trah-nee-shah)	-	Healing grace
Trashonna (tra-shon-nah)	-	Finding God's presence
Trenette (tren-et)	-	I am prosperity
Trenyce (tren-e-s)	-	Power of love
Tri (try)	-	To enter into wisdom
Tricia (trih-she-ah)	-	Creative power
Trina (tree-nah)	-	To acknowledge God
Trista (tris-tah)	-	In the will of God
T'Shura (t-sure-ah)	-	God's peace
TuKisha (tu-ke-sha)	-	Life of grace
Tundalisa (tun-dah-lee-sah)	-	To expect the best
Tundolaya (tun-doe-lie-ah)	-	To hear God
Tusajigwe' (too-sah-jig-way)	-	We are blessed

Twana (t'won-ah)   -   Faith filled
Tyeasa (ty-e-sah)   -   Rich child of God
Tyese (ty-eese)   -   Wisdom of spirit
Tyeya (tay-yah)   -   Honoring God's love
Tyra (ty-rah)   -   To speak faith
T'Ziah (t'zy-ah)   -   Understanding goodness
Takombra (tah-comb-rah)   -   Abundant good

U

Uisha (u-e-sha)   -   To sing praises
Ulani (u-lon-e)   -   To radiate peace
Umeah (u-me-ah)   -   Multiplied blessings
Uncilla (un-cilla)   -   My Lord
Undrea (un-dray-ah)   -   Patient and kind
Uneah (u-ne-ah)   -   Vibrant flower
Unesha (u-ne-sha)   -   Coming to hear God
Unis (you-nis)   -   Protecting shield
Unity (you-nih-t)   -   The way of love
Uniqua (you-nee-quah)   -   Life of joy
Unosha (u-no-sha)   -   Christ presence
Unyiah (u-ny-ah)   -   To seek God's presence
Ureatha (u-ree-tha)   -   Armour of God
Uronia (u-roe-ne-ah)   -   My heart sings
Ursena (ur-see-nah)   -   One with God
Ursula (ur-su-lah)   -   Limitless wealth
Usentra (u-sen-tra)   -   Harmonizing power of God

V

Valencia (va-len-see-ah)   -   New life
Vanatta (va-nah-tah)   -   Principal centered
Vanessa (va-nes-sah)   -   To find truth
Vanetha (vah-ne-tha)   -   Oneness
Vanisha (vah-nih-sha)   -   Unity

Vanshell (van-shell)	-	Word of God
Venetia (ven-eht-ah)	-	Perfect demonstration
Venezia (ven-e-z-ah)	-	Truth in God
Venus (ve-nus)	-	Building love
Verenda (ver-en-dah)	-	Glorifying the lord
Vermilia (ver-mil-e-ah)	-	I let God guide
Veronica (verr-on-nih-kah)	-	Infinite wisdom
Veronique (verr-on-neek)	-	Finding grace with God
Versaous (ver-say-ous)	-	Have faith
Versie (ver-sy)	-	Child of light
Veverlyn (veh-ver-lyn)	-	God's instrument
Vichelle (vih-shell)	-	A new beginning
Vicita (vih-see-tah)	-	The perfect way
Vickia (vick-e-ah)	-	Covering God's word
Vicondra (vih-con-dra)	-	Creative mind
Victoria (vic-tory-ah)	-	God's victory
Vinera (vin-er-ah)	-	Rich storehouse
Vinisha (vin-ih-sha)	-	To bless all
Viniqua (vin-e-quah)	-	Permanent prosperity
Vishondra (vih-shon-dra)	-	Limitless power
Vivian (vih-ve-an)	-	Divine wisdom
Vivica (vih-vih-kah)	-	Divine supply
Vondella (von-del-ah)	-	Poised in faith
Voncella (von-cell-ah)	-	Divine source
Vonita (von-e-tah)	-	To demonstrate supply
Vonzell (von-zell)	-	Pursuing faith in God
Vonzetta (von-zet-ah)	-	To love always
Voshell (vo-shell)	-	Calm waves
VoShawn (vo-shon)	-	To call on God

W

Walitha (wah-lee-tha)	-	Great strength in God
Walunda (wah-lun-dah)	-	Sharing love
Wanda (won-dah)	-	Creative nature

Wanesha (wah-nee-sha)	-	To think confidently
Wahena (wah-he-nah)	-	God's wisdom
Waris (war-is)	-	African spirit
Warrika (war-e-kah)	-	Living spirit
Washika (wah-she-kah)	-	Giving thanks
Wayota (way-o-tah)	-	God's channel
Wendolyn (wen-doe-lyn)	-	Winds of faith
Wendy (wen-dee)	-	Wings of love
Whitney (whit-nee)	-	Feeling saved
Winnie (win-e)	-	God's action
Wintress (win-tress)	-	Great love of God
Wishawn (wih-shon)	-	United with God
Wishelle (wih-shell)	-	Good comes to me
Wishena (wih-she-nah)	-	God is within me
Wonada (won-ah-dah)	-	spiritual presence
Wonetta (won-eh-tah)	-	Precious gift
Wyella (wy-ella)	-	Power to heal
Wycina (wy-see-nah)	-	To think joyfully
Wynona (wy-no-nah)	-	Sustained faith

X

Xavia (x-a-v-ah)	-	Supreme creation
Xavier (x-a-v-er)	-	Unlimited supply
Xena (x-e-nah)	-	To dwell on God
Xenthia (x-en-thee-ah)	-	Boundless good

Y

Yanetta (yah-net-ah)	-	To know God
Yania (yah-nee-ah)	-	God prospers me
Yapheta (yah-phet-ah)	-	Perfect image
Yasmine (yas-min)	-	Perfectly made
Yavina (yah-vee-nah)	-	To stand on faith
Yavinia (yah-vin-e-ah)	-	To relax in spirit

Yohanna (yo-han-ah)   -   Great strength
Yolanda (yo-lon-dah)   -   To surrender all
Yontel (yon-tell)   -   Finishing great things
Yonzetta (yon-zetta)   -   Feeling righteous in God
Yumika (you-me-kah)   -   Tender hearted
Yushonda (you-shon-dah)   -   Finding Strength
Yvandra (e-von-dra)   -   One who is worthy
Yvette (e-vet)   -   To accept the blessings
Yvonne (e-von)   -   God provides

Z

Zamika (zah-me-kah)   -   To be open
Zana (zay-nah)   -   Positive feeling
Zara (zah-rah)   -   Fearless faith
Zaynah (zay-nah)   -   Long awaited joy
Zelia (ze-lee-ah)   -   Loving nature
Zenobia (zen-o-bee-ah)   -   Expression of God
Zetta (zet-ah)   -   Blessed by God
Zimetria (zim-e-tree-ah)   -   To build consciousness
Zina (zee-nah)   -   Joyous life
Ziphoena (zih-phee-nah)   -   Sweet natured
Zisharra (zih-sha-rah)   -   To accomplish much
Zipporah (zih-por-rah)   -   Open to love
Zisheena (zih-she-nah)   -   Finding beauty in God
Zoria (zor-e-ah)   -   Charged with love
Zori (zor-e)   -   Heavens gift